Perfect Souls Shine Through

A PERSONAL PHOTO DOCUMENTARY OF THE EVENTS SURROUNDING SEPTEMBER 11, 2001

PHOTOGRAPHY AND STORY

EDWARD J. WHITEHEAD

TEXT

KEN HONEYWELL

DESIGN

PATRICIA PRATHER

GALYAN'S, PLAINFIELD, INDIANA

For all those touched by the events of 9/11/01

This book was created through the generous donation of time, talent, materials, services, and support from the following individuals and companies.

SPECIAL THANKS:

Ken Honeywell for writing

Patricia Prather, Bruce Dean, Scott Johnson, and the entire Dean Johnson Design staff for design and layout

Vertis, Inc. for print production, scans, planning and execution

Graphic Communications for paper and freight

Lake Book Manufacturing for binding

David Lehr, Jeff Morden, Robert Burch, Hee Jun, and everyone on the GALYAN'S team for direction and coordination

J&H Display for displays

Carey Digital for banners

ICE MILLER for legal services

On Monday, September 10, the world was perfect.

NOT REALLY PERFECT. BUT THERE WERE PARTS OF MY world that seemed perfect that afternoon, a clear and beautiful day I spent at the beach in Amagansett with my best friends James and Robert, along with Robert's wife, Mary, and their four-year-old twins, Sophia and Griffin. The beach was uncrowded, the summer people having long since left the Hamptons to resume their lives as bankers and brokers and publishing executives. We nearly had the ocean to ourselves. I was surrounded by my best friends, perfect weather, the ocean, and two beautiful children. It all seemed idyllic. With camera in hand, I began to document the day for us to remember in those years ahead when our memories will have faded.

There was also a not-so-perfect part of my world at the time: earlier in the year, my sister had been in a near-fatal automobile accident and had been in a coma for several months. I had come home to take care of her and I was splitting my time between her house in South Carolina and my apartment in Greenwich Village. My apartment's bedroom window looked south down Sixth Avenue, perfectly framing the Twin Towers of the World Trade Center.

I enjoyed living in the Village. Although I'd actually been born in Washington, D.C., and had grown up in Advance, North Carolina, a peaceful town near Winston-Salem, I'd lived in big cities for most of my adult life. I'd worked in Manhattan and London and Southern California, and I enjoyed the lifestyle. I loved the pace of the city life, restaurants, music, and the sounds of the street.

That day at the beach, I felt as if these were the best pictures I had ever taken. The twins were innocent and beautiful, and they knew and trusted me, so they were entirely at ease, entirely unguarded for the camera. It felt like a natural extension of my mind's eye. The world was turning as it should.

Less than eighteen hours later, the world would suddenly seem to stop turning for one awful moment, and then for another, and then start spinning wildly in the opposite direction. My camera would become not an extension of me, but an emotional reservoir that allowed me to capture some of the madness, the terror, and the indescribable and indomitable spirit of people coming to grips with a world that was suddenly, utterly, irrevocably changed. Truly, I did not understand until very late in my photographic odyssey just how much emotion I'd allowed to imprint itself on the film in my camera, but not on my heart. When I put down the camera, I found, to my great surprise, that the lenses through which I'd viewed the world had only delayed my emotional response: it was all inside me, and I was overcome. My life had changed right along with everyone else's.

It is difficult for me to know how to talk about September 11 and the weeks that followed. It seems somehow inappropriate

to suggest that I was fortunate to be there in Lower Manhattan, with cameras and lenses and forty rolls of film and nothing to do but walk the streets and take photographs. But in a way, I do feel tremendously fortunate to have been able to document things few others saw, and to do so not as a trained photojournalist, but as an amateur, somebody not too much different from a tourist with a disposable camera. Sometimes, it's not the posed portraits or well-framed landscapes that inspire and move you, but the snapshots of average people at extraordinary moments. In this way, the photos of the remarkable events and the people I encountered in the aftermath of September 11 are not much different from the photos of Sophia and Griffin. The circumstances were very nearly opposite.

But the perfect souls shine through.

The Towers

WHERE WERE YOU WHEN YOU HEARD ABOUT THE plane hitting the tower? I had just left my apartment to walk up Sixth Avenue to grab a cup of coffee and read the newspaper, as had been my routine most mornings. I glanced at my watch as I closed my apartment door: 8:45 a.m.

By the time the elevator delivered me to the lobby of my building, it was 8:48. The first plane had hit the south tower.

On the street, you couldn't see much difference yet. People hustled past to work. Traffic was heavy, as usual. The weather was bright and clear, as the day before had been. But I noticed that a few people were standing in pockets on the sidewalk, looking southward into the air. One of them was a policeman.

"What's going on, officer?" I asked.

"Plane hit the World Trade Center," he said.

My first thought, like most people's, was that this was some kind of bizarre accident. Some pilot not paying attention or having a heart attack. It had been a small plane, surely; that was what it looked like from this distance, the black-and-red scar and the billowing smoke still dwarfed by the massive Twin Towers. Shocking. But, really: weren't we all a little surprised that this had never happened before?

The emergency vehicles began to scream throughout the city. More people stopped to watch as the plume of smoke rose higher in the blue September sky.

And then, standing there on Sixth Avenue, I saw the second plane hit. And we knew none of it was an accident.

I'm not sure why, but I went back upstairs to my apartment. The first photos I took of the towers on fire were shot from my bedroom window. I watched in horrified awe and listened with one ear to the television I'd turned on in the other room—listened as the dignified and unflappable Peter Jennings' reserve crumbled in the face of an unprecedented act of terrorism that was still unfolding. Reports were coming in from Washington. The Pentagon had been hit, perhaps the White House. Other planes were missing. The sirens grew louder. People below me stood on rooftops and patios and stared into the distance.

The world was spinning in reverse.

My phone rang. It was one of my nephews from Washington, D.C. who wanted to make sure I was okay. I was describing the incredible spectacle for him when the first tower collapsed in a horrific cloud of smoke and the phone line went dead.

Suddenly, I knew it was time for me to get to the street. I can't explain, I just knew. I grabbed my gear and every roll of film I could find and left my apartment.

Out on the street, people shouted, wept, paced, sat in stunned silence, hands wrapped around their heads. I encountered a woman covered from head to foot with dust. "I was on the seventy-fourth floor," she said. "They told us to stay calm, but I didn't stay calm. I left."

An elderly woman approached me, her face blank. "Excuse me," she said. "I'm really afraid, I don't know what to do. Can you tell me where I should go?"

I told her there was a church a couple of blocks away, and that maybe she could go there. This seemed to hearten her, provide her with a sense of purpose.

As for myself, I heard they needed blood at St. Vincent's Hospital, the closest hospital to what we would, in the days ahead, begin to call Ground Zero. It was a short walk away, and I made my way there.

The first photos I took of the towers on fire were shot from my bedroom window.

More people stopped to watch as the plume of **smoke rose** higher in the blue September sky.

People below me stood on rooftops and patios and stared into the distance.

Out on the street, people **shout**
silence, hands **wrapped** around

ed, wept, paced, **sat** in stunned
their **heads**.

"Excuse me," she said. "I'm really afraid, I don't know what to do. Can you tell me where I should go?"

St. Vincent's Hospital

ALONG THE WAY TO THE HOSPITAL, I BEGAN TO SEE strange and remarkable things, as if they could become any stranger or more remarkable. Here, less than an hour after it had all begun, was a homeless man whose hand-lettered sign asking for help was already counterbalanced with another asking for prayer for the victims. Here was a lone man in an *I Love New York* tee shirt engulfed in morning shadows. Here were boxes of flares and piles of batons and helmets and other police gear lying in the street, untouched.

This was the truly unnerving part of the hours just following the collapse of the towers: the police and federal agents were just as confused, just as lost and shocked, as the rest of us. That, and the view down Sixth Avenue, one of New York's busiest thoroughfares, was empty of traffic and terminated in a cloud of smoke.

St. Vincent's Hospital on West 12th Street in Greenwich Village was a staging area for a lot of different interests—medical, media, police, rescue, and others—and a gathering place for people wondering what they could do to help. By the time I arrived around 11 a.m., every tree and light pole, every television van, was already being covered with flyers bearing the likenesses of people who may have been down at the towers, and the blood donation line was already several blocks long. By 2 p.m., the hospital had run out of equipment for drawing blood.

And the shocking reality at that point was that there was not going to be a lot of need for blood. Hospital orderlies lined up rows of clean, white beds outside, waiting for casualties that never arrived. We were all waiting for casualties, for some sign that there were people down there who were all right. The sign never came.

I met my friends James and Christina at the hospital, and we hugged and reassured each other of our love and friendship. We waited there and listened to the rumors circulating among the crowd, uncertain of what to believe. But with all the people gathered here, we felt oddly safe, so we stayed.

At one point, a buzz began rippling through the crowd, as if someone important had arrived. The crowd parted, and a contingent of ironworkers walked through. These, I could not help but think, were the men who looked like heroes: strong, clear-eyed, ready to go to work. They instilled some hope in all of us, I believe, that someone was in charge, someone could make a difference.

This was the truly unnerving part of the hours just following the collapse of the towers:
the police and federal agents were just as confused, just as lost and shocked, as the rest of us.

Waiting . . .

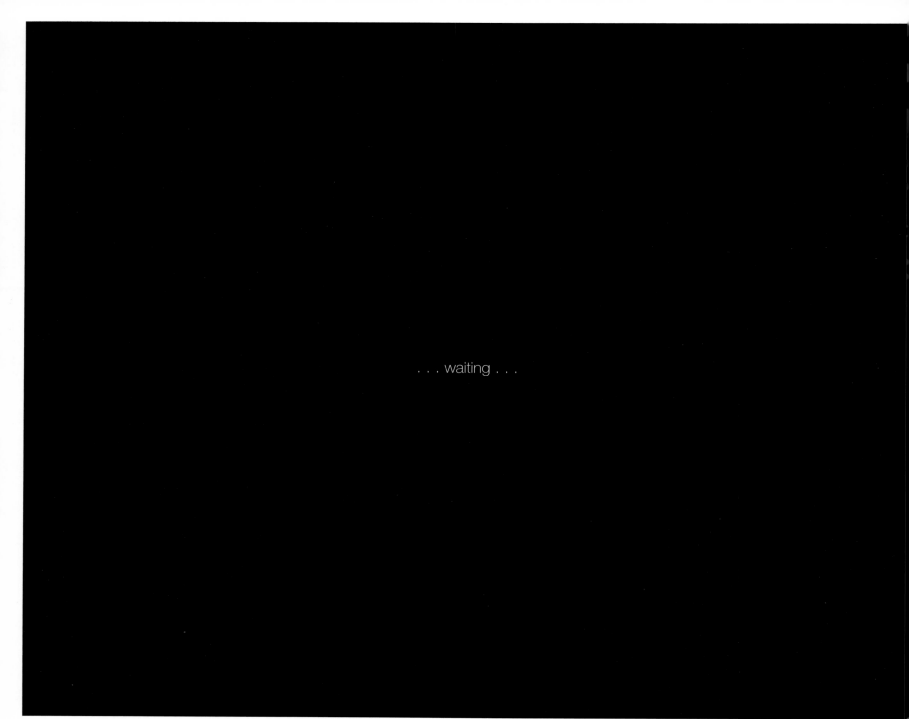

. . . waiting . . .

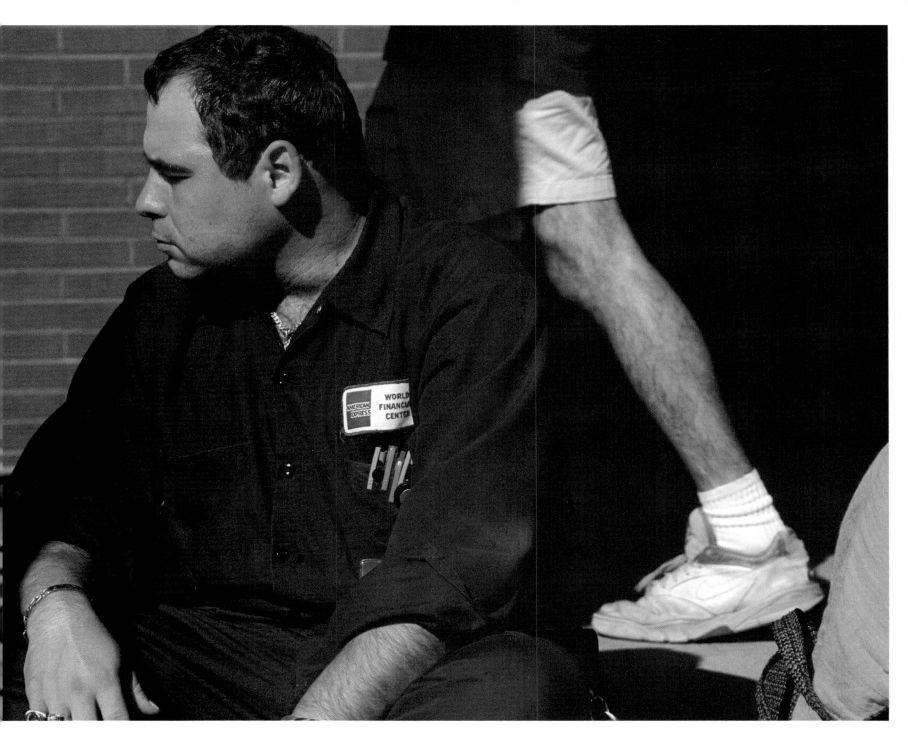

. . . still waiting.

These . . . were the men who looked like **heroes** . . .

. . . **strong**, clear-eyed, **ready** to go to work.

Union Square Park

AFTER I LEFT THE HOSPITAL, I WENT HOME TO REST and try to eat something. But I couldn't stay in my apartment that evening. The television news was full of speculation and sadness and outrage, but very little of substance that we hadn't known for hours. I grabbed my gear and decided to head to Union Square Park, a natural gathering place in the center of the city. I had no idea whether anything would be going on there, but I figured it was a logical place to look.

I wasn't disappointed. The park was crowded with people of all ages, races, and creeds in an assembly that seemed part war protest, part peace rally, part civil rights convention, part Grateful Dead concert. At one end of the park, people waved handmade signs and debated—not angrily, but passionately—the events of the day and what our nation's response and our personal responsibilities should be. At the other end, someone had laid out a huge arrangement of candles in the shape of a peace symbol and draped an enormous, swirling peace blanket across the steps. Two men with a large format Polaroid camera were taking photos of people and pasting them to an oversized poster on which they had constructed the word "Faith" out of black tape, and allowed their subjects to write their own captions for their pictures.

Also down by the peace symbol-end of the park was a large group playing music. This was not any sort of band, but rather an impromptu concert by people who had brought their guitars and drums and horns to the park to make healing noises. To say they all played together would be less accurate than to say they all played at the same time. The effect was tribal and hypnotic, and the crowd swayed and danced as if possessed.

I spent many hours at Union Square Park that week. The sea of candles and flowers and signs grew day by day, until it overflowed the boundaries of the park.

The park was **crowded** with people
rally, part civil **rights** convention,

. . . part war **protest**, part **peace** part Grateful Dead **concert**.

Someone had laid out a huge arrangement of candles in the shape of a peace symbol and draped an enormous, swirling peace blanket across the steps.

Westside Highway

THAT SAME NIGHT—ACTUALLY, WHAT HAD LONG SINCE become the morning of September 12—I made my way to the Westside Highway, which I'd heard had become another gathering place. I stayed for a while, but I didn't have any more film in my bag, so I went home and, while exhausted both physically and emotionally, got only a few restless hours' sleep.

I returned to the Westside Highway the next morning with my friend Robert. The city had closed the highway to all traffic except emergency and support vehicles to and from Ground Zero. People lined the median between the north and southbound lanes, cheering for the firefighters and ironworkers, the police, even the trucks ferrying drinking water to the site of the devastation: cheers for the crews headed to the scene, cheers for the tired workers coming back the other way. Some cheered openly, vocally, almost raucously. Some waved banners or held up silent peace sign salutes. Everyone had something to say, and, as diverse as the crowd was, the message was clear, unified: take care of yourself, we support you, we love you.

Sometimes, the reactions along the road were very personal. On September 12, I watched a young firefighter stare down the highway in grim anticipation, wondering whether his buddies were living or dead. When he saw their truck, he threw his arms into the air, overcome with joy.

Not all workers from Ground Zero returned on the Westside Highway in trucks. Many times, I saw firefighters and other rescue workers walking away from Ground Zero alone, many blocks from the site. I could only imagine their need for that long walk to try and create some separation for themselves between the horror they had experienced and the rest of their lives.

The **message** was clear, unified: take care of yourself, we support you, **we love you**.

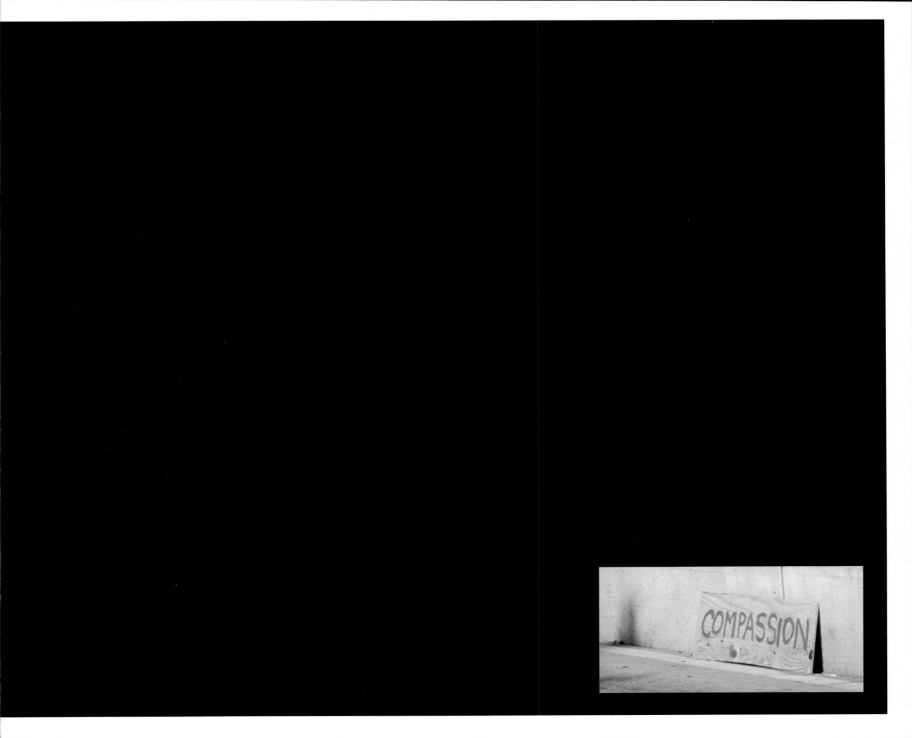

When he saw their truck, he threw his arms into the air, overcome with joy.

I can only imagine their need for that long walk . . .

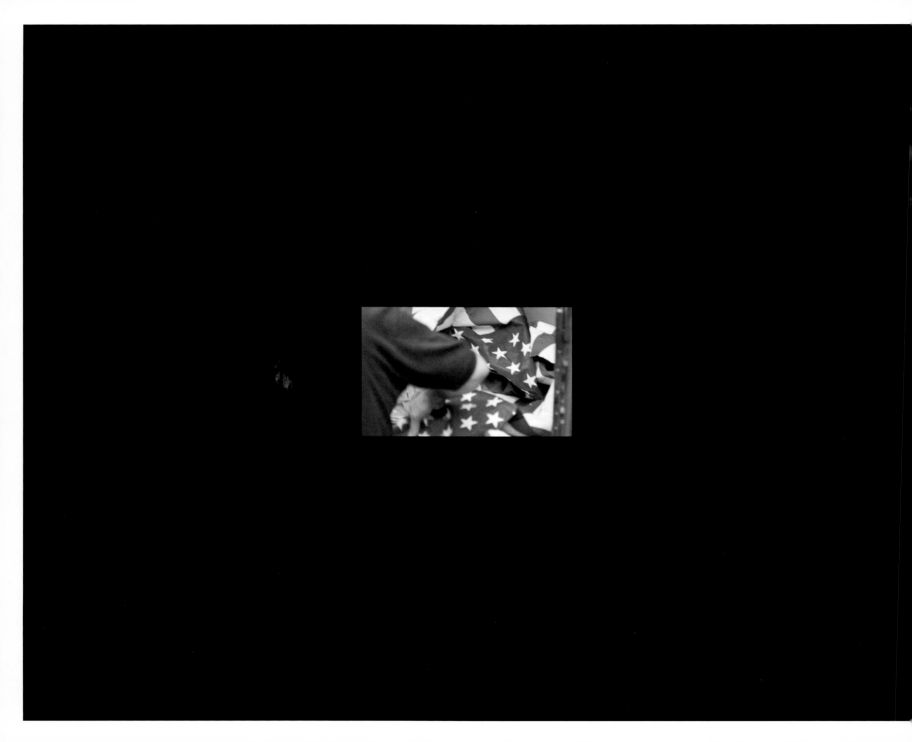

Flag Salesman

ONE MORNING, A MAN WITH A VANLOAD OF FLAGS arrived in the Village. These were cheap, printed flags he was selling for four dollars apiece. Before he'd fastened his money belt, he had buyers lined up halfway down the block.

I could not help but be struck by the irony of the situation. This was exactly what the terrorist attacks had been calculated to strike against: the flag, the commerce. It was easy to be a bit taken aback by the idea of a man profiting from this tragedy, selling flags out of the back of a van. Still, he had a commodity people wanted—something they needed. He could have sold them for forty dollars apiece, and if he'd had ten thousand of them, he'd have sold them all.

It's no great revelation that the flag was everywhere in those days after the attacks, but the ways you saw the flag employed were always interesting. People used flags as shawls and capes and neckerchiefs. I encountered one man in a jumpsuit made of flags, standing on the sidewalk and orating passionately in Italian. I don't know a word of Italian, but my takeaway was that he'd left Italy to get away from this sort of thing, and he was not going to let terrorists run him out of his home. He was fiercely American and proud to be so. I could only wonder whether he'd made his flag suit in response to the attacks or it was something he just liked to wear from time to time.

It's no great revelation that the **flag was everywhere** in those days after the attacks . . .

. . . he wasn't going to let terrorists run him out of his home.

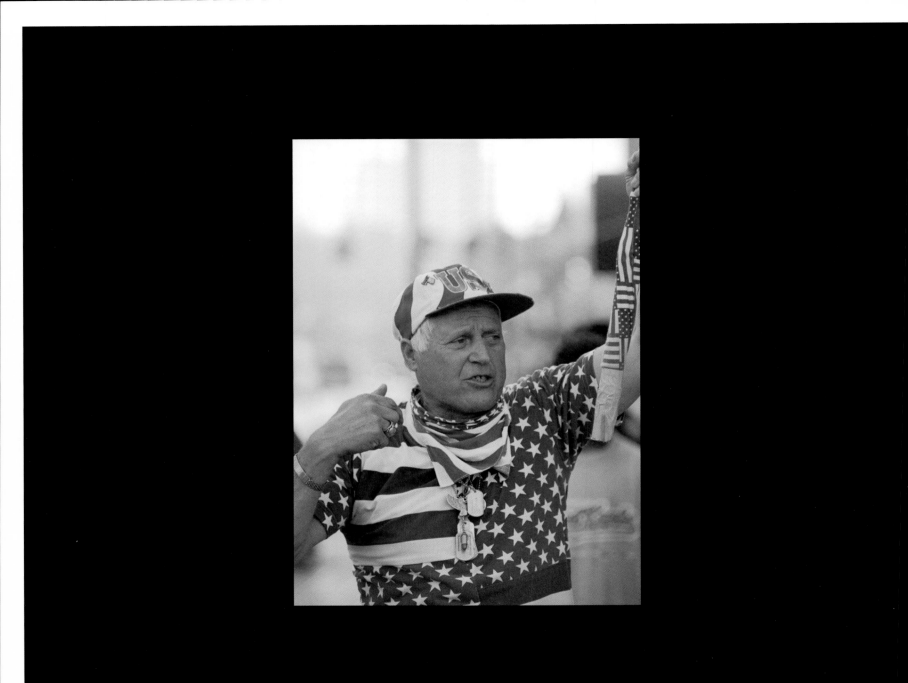

City Scenes

THE IMAGES AROUND THE CITY GREW WITH EACH day. The normal sights where no longer normal. Or, at least it seemed that way. Everything seemed to be cast in a different light, framed in a different context.

Washington Square Park is one of those places you've seen a thousand times in movies shot in Manhattan: the heart of Greenwich Village, close by New York University, a huge central fountain, men playing chess. It was another place people gravitated after the attacks, a place where people came to be around other people, and I passed through many times on my way around the city.

Unlike Union Square Park, Washington Square Park was anything but raucous. It was unusually quiet. The park was filled with music—lots of guitar playing and singing, very little talking. It was also another place filled with makeshift, temporary monuments: flowers, candles, replicas of the Twin Towers with row upon row of tiny windows painstakingly cut out. Around one of the park's permanent statues, a chain-link fence had been erected by workers doing repairs. The fence became a wall of photos and posters covered with signatures and admonitions to faith and prayer and tolerance.

Nights in the city were particularly eerie. The enormous shroud of smoke, so evident during the day, became positively ghostly when illuminated by the lights of the city at night. An acrid scent like nothing I had ever smelled before hung in the air. I imagined it to be the smell of war.

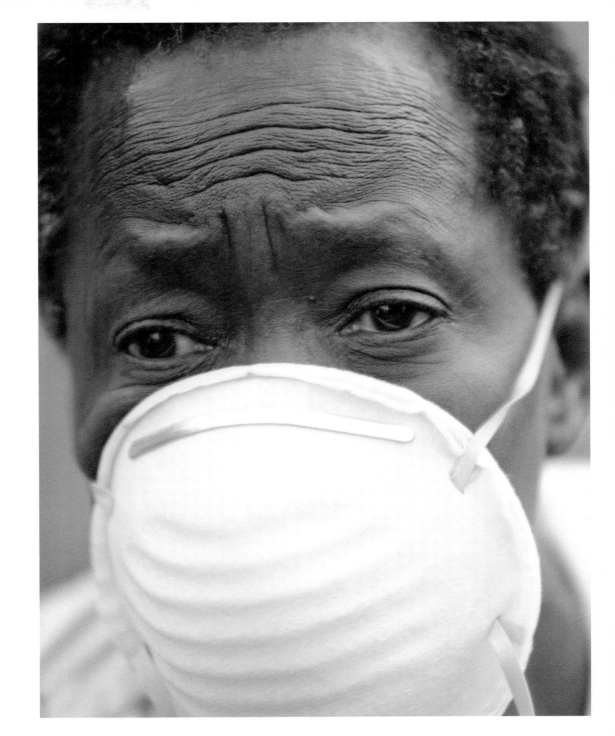

Nights in the city were particularly eerie.

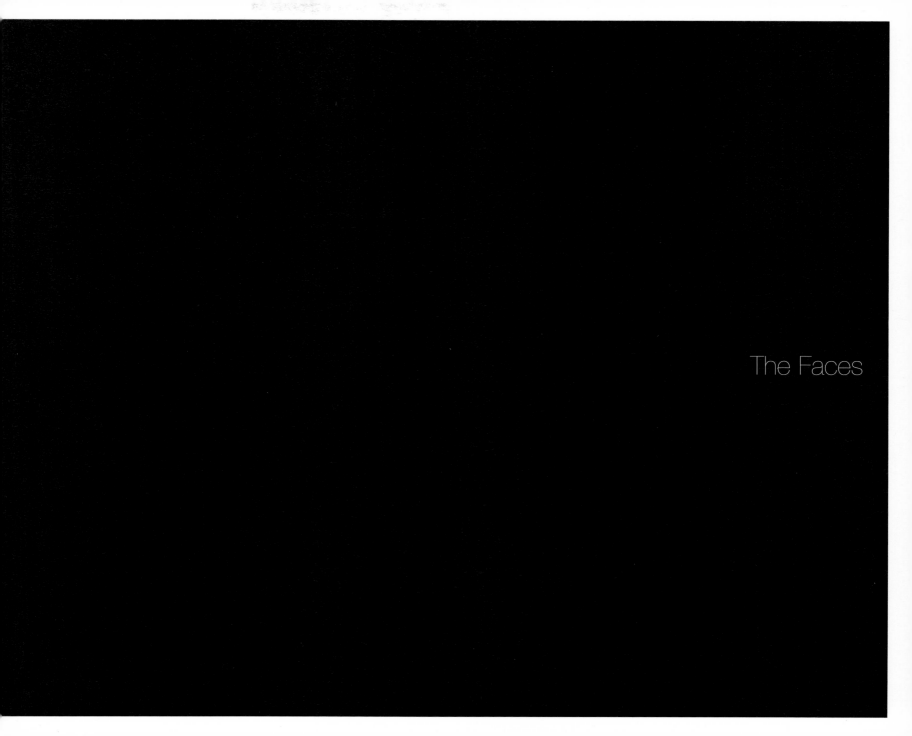

The Faces

JOE TROMBINO
(FRANCES) BRINKS GUARD
973-478-8640
MISSING
JOE TROMBINO
(FRANCES) CO-WORKERS CALL HIM JAC
BRINKS GUARD
LAST SEEN 9:15 AM TUES
PARKING GARAGE TOWER /
WITH BRINKS TRUCK
ANY INFO CALL
973-478-8640
PLEASE !!

I SAW A LOT OF REMARKABLE THINGS ON THE STREETS in the weeks following the attacks. Just outside Union Square Park, I first encountered a man walking the streets carrying an enormous cross that was covered with writing and raggedy cloths. I saw him many times, at many different places around the city, and I never saw him talk with anyone. He did not appear to be doing this to impress anyone. It was simply his burden.

You could not walk anywhere in the city without seeing the faces of people missing in lower Manhattan; within hours of the attacks, posters bearing their photos and descriptions were being distributed and attached to anything that stood still. I would venture a guess that nearly everyone who vanished was represented by one of these posters.

There were so many different faces on the flyers that one could think the effort was almost self-defeating: they looked like a large and randomly selected sampling of all the people of the world, no different from the people you'd see on a subway car or walking around Times Square after the theaters let out. But as the days went by, you got to know the faces. You began to imagine their lives. You knew personal things about them from the text on the posters: what their co-workers called them, what kind of clothing they wore. One woman in particular, a beautiful young woman who'd worked for Cantor Fitzgerald, seemed to follow me wherever I went.

Increasingly, I understood that I was looking at ghosts. These people were not going to be found alive, and perhaps would never be found at all. Their secondary effect became primary. "Know me," the posters said. "This is who I was. Remember me."

. . . I was looking at ghosts.

This is who I was. Remember me.

I saw him many times . . .

. . . at many different places . . .

Division 1 Fire Station

YOU CAN BARELY TURN A CORNER IN NEW YORK CITY without running into a fire station. To me, they had always been hubs of activity, neighborhood anchors. The firefighters lived with the prospect of danger every day, but they had nice lives, as well. Their doors were always open, their gleaming engines on display for passersby. Their reward for risking their lives was that they also got to spend hours watching the pretty girls on the sidewalks, and this did not seem like such a bad job to me.

In the aftermath of the terrorist attacks, New York's fire stations became very different places. They became shrines to fallen heroes, places of quiet reverence. The firefighters did not stand outside and joke with the tourists. Their doors were no longer open; there was too much grief, too much shocking loss, and when they were not doing the terrible work of helping clear rubble and search for victims—and perform their day-to-day duties for the rest of the city—they pulled in and took care of themselves.

On the last day I took photographs in the city, I stopped at Division 1, my neighborhood station in Greenwich Village. It was a contingent that had been especially devastated in the attack, having lost eleven of its own. Evidence of the firefighters' grief and their pride in fallen comrades was everywhere, from the posters and candles and flowers lining the building to the pickup truck, a vehicle that had endured a heavy beating in the crash of the towers, to which had been welded the side panel of one of the fire trucks that had been otherwise destroyed.

After I took some shots outside, the station's door opened and I asked a young firefighter if I might come inside for a moment. He agreed. The place was as quiet as a cathedral. I took a couple of shots—one of an assemblage of gear hanging beneath a large American flag that made my hands shake—and I left.

Back out on the street, a huge dump truck, its bed filled with rubble, was paused in front of the station. In the cab sat a hard man, his face dirty and streaked with sweat; obviously, he had just come from Ground Zero. I looked at him, and he looked at me. "Thank you," I mouthed silently. He nodded, and we both began to weep, both of us overcome by a tragedy we had lived with for weeks that was suddenly too much for us.

I decided it was time to walk where I had not walked. I walked south to Ground Zero. In the previous days, there was nothing I could have done to help there, and I hadn't wanted to get in anyone's way. And perhaps I really didn't want to see it.

I saw it then. Here was the rubble and the devastation, the monstrous pile still smoking, the acrid taste still hanging in the air. I took one photo and walked back to my apartment. I had seen enough.

Evidence of the firefighter's grief and their pride in fallen comrades was everywhere . . .

TO OUR BROTHERS
WE LOVE YOU ALL
BC Bill McGovern
BC Richard Prunty
LT Vinny Giammona
LT Mike Warchola
FF John Santore
FF ommy Hannafin
FF reg Saucedo
FF Paul Keating
FF Louie Arena
FF Andy Brunn
FF Faustino Apostol
GOD BLESS FDNY

. . . obviously a vehicle that had endured a heavy beating in the crash of the towers . . .

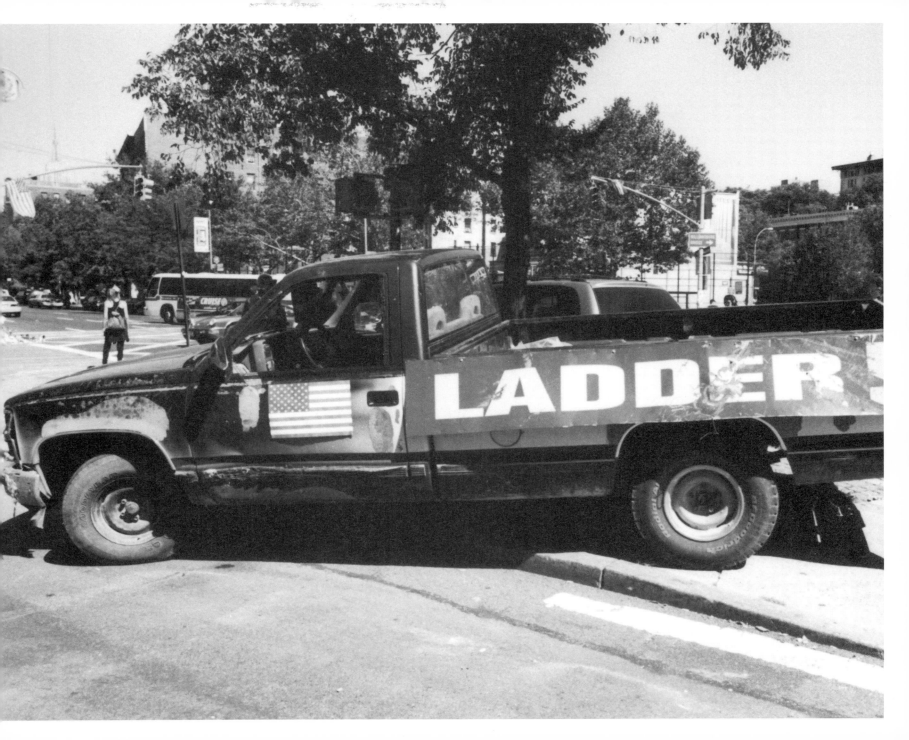

I walked south to Ground Zero.

I had seen enough.

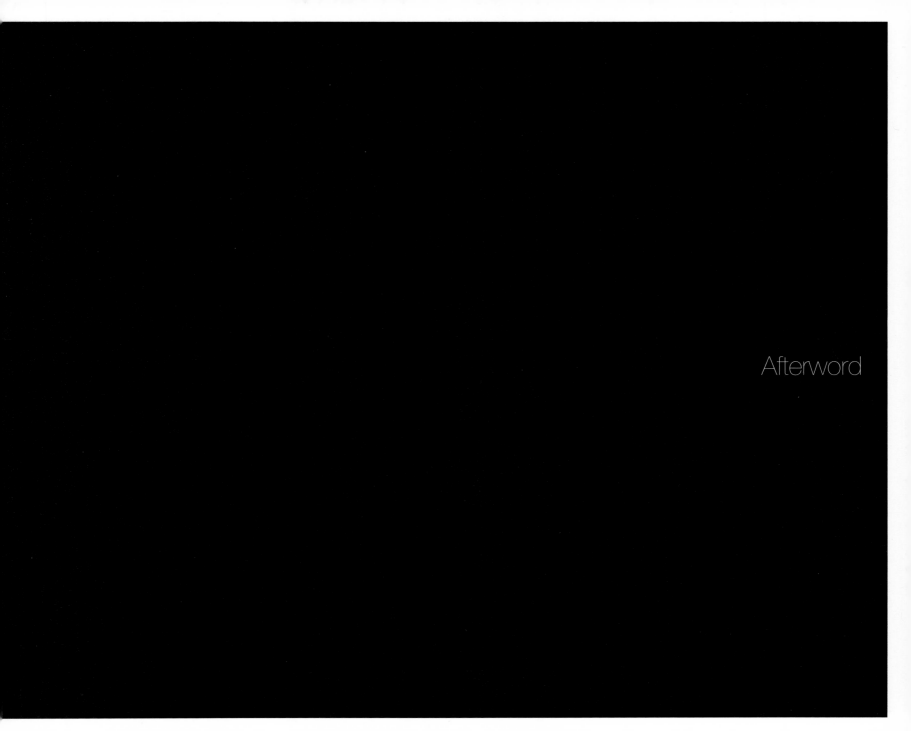

Afterword

SEVERAL WEEKS PASSED BEFORE I DEVELOPED THE film I shot in Manhattan. When I received the prints, I was shocked to realize that there, on the same roll of film, were the two poles of my story: the twins, Sophia and Griffin, playing on the beach in the late summer sun; the Twin Towers of the World Trade Center crumbling like sand castles. It was as if the most beautiful and difficult things in my life had become, if not inter-twined, at least set side by side for my consideration.

And so I considered my life, as I expect we all did. In the aftermath of September 11, we no longer see skyscrapers or airplanes with the same eyes, or police officers or firefighters. Or the people we love.

Today, my sister is out of the hospital and in recovery. She can walk and talk and see, and those are all small miracles. She still has many challenges and she is different from the person I grew up with—but she is my sister, my family, and my love for

her has deepened. We are closer now than we ever have been.

A lot of other things changed in my life, too, among them my definition of success. My life had been a success by all conventional American standards: jobs that took me to the world's most important cities, fancy addresses, all the material comfort one could hope for. I learned first-hand that it was all replaceable. The only things that really mattered were the things you couldn't replace: the people you loved, and your love for them. I'm certainly not the first person to be a witness to destruction and come away with this thought, but the unoriginality of it makes it no less true or powerful.

Soon after I stopped taking pictures in Manhattan, I had the extraordinary good fortune to find a new job in the Midwest, to work and live in a city that is remarkable both for what it has and what it does not have. I sometimes feel as if this place is my secret, that I have found the place that has allowed me to return to the values of my childhood. It is a place I wasn't sure existed anymore.

In a way, though, I think our whole world has become a rediscovered place since September 11, 2001. We have all taken to seeing each other through new eyes, all learned to value things differently, all begun once again to embrace what is real and lasting in our lives.

I have heard it said that, if you talk with cancer patients several years after their disease is in remission and ask them how their lives have changed, you would almost think something wonderful had happened to them. They make changes in their lives they would never have made had they not been afflicted with a life-threatening disease that shook them to their foundations.

I cannot say the world is better for what happened in Lower Manhattan on that terrible day. I can say that my life has been transformed, and that my life is better, in part because of how I responded to the things that happened there. This, I think, is what I owe to the people who lost their lives and the millions of others who are still affected by the people and the events of September 11—and, not least of all, my sister and James, Robert and Mary, Sophia and Griffin, and all the wonderful people who have touched my life: a commitment to living fearlessly and loving the best way I know how.